MW01533354

Zack -
I love your story -
Be you -
Your Perfect -
Always
Collette

Annie Finds Her Magic

"Helen Keller's teacher tells her story."

Collette Cullen

Copyright © 2015 Collette Cullen

All rights reserved

ISBN-13: 978-1499571172
ISBN-10: 1499571178

Annie Finds Her Magic

is dedicated to...

all teachers

sung and unsung.

Reviews

Collette Cullen's "Annie" channels the unbridled spirit and boundless love of Annie Sullivan, pioneering educator and personal teacher of Helen Keller, the world's most famous disabled student. Cullen gives voice to Sullivan's soul, sharing her triumphant and true-life story, and the inspiring journey Sullivan takes to conquer her own disabilities. Steeled by her personal battles, Sullivan develops the strength and courage to school the "unteachable Keller" and unlock the "magic" trapped inside her. It is Sullivan's perseverance that releases Keller from the bondage of blindness and deafness.

"Annie" speaks to us with childlike candor and a "spitfire" personality to prove that love indeed conquers all. Every teacher and student should read this book, and then dream.

Chris Stepien, author of "Three Days: The Search for the Boy Messiah"

This unique book tells the untold story of Annie Sullivan, teacher of Helen Keller. It will inspire readers of all ages to plug into the magic of writing as they tell their own stories.

Mary Allen, author of "The Rooms of Heaven."

Collette Cullen's children's book, *Annie Finds Her Magic*, is a detailed, delightful and richly woven biography of Helen Keller's brilliant teacher, Anne Sullivan. But it is much more than that. It is an exploration of possibility, of discovery, and of determination. While it informs young readers about the life of this extraordinary woman and her remarkable student, it also challenges them to think deeply about their own lives. While it explores Sullivan's gifts, it asks children to consider what *their* special gifts are.

Jill Jepson, author of "Writing as a Sacred Path: A Practical Guide to Writing with Passion and Purpose."

Acknowledgements

Helen Keller said that the day she met her teacher, Annie Sullivan was the day her "souls birthday."

This comment inspired me to study Annie Sullivan, to create my one-woman performance as Annie and to ultimately write this book. In the process there have been people who have been my inspiration and support, perhaps they were my soul's teachers. They are the "invisible hands" that in every way shaped this book helping me to believe when I feared I might falter.

I am indebted to and grateful to so many. In particular, Judy Arkwright, Anne Gautreau, Rosa Scaramucci, Liz Rohan, Cindy Frabutt, Shirley Damps and Cindy Frankel, these generous women shared expansively of their talents and time.

Also a very special thanks to Jillian Drapala whose lovely images and effervescent energy helped me to imagine the heart the young teacher, Annie Sullivan.

Lastly thank you to all those who held candles to my darkness and helped make a believer out of me. As Annie says, "dream big.

Chapter 1

Can someone live forever? What do you think?

I am a teacher. My name is Annie Sullivan.

I was born on April 14, 1866 in Feeding Hills, Massachusetts.

I am famous. Some say, I am the most famous teacher in American History. I am famous for being Helen Keller's teacher. Do you know who Helen Keller was? She was a girl who was deaf and blind.

Helen was one of the first people ever to learn to speak with her hands, signing. Signing is the same as talking, but it is done with fingers.

This is a way for deaf people to communicate. Their fingers create voice, words.

In those times, back in the 1860's, before Helen was born, life was pretty terrible for deaf and blind people. I know this myself, since I was mostly blind.

I sure was proud of Helen. At that time in history, there were no schools for children who were different. I was not allowed in school. Why, you ask?

Children, who were handicapped, different from others, often lived in state run hospitals, places that were like jails. Sometimes people lived their entire lives there.

Helen's mother did not want to send her little girl away. She believed that Helen could learn. Helen struggled. Being blind and deaf, with no way of talking, she had no way to tell her mother what she wanted.

Helen's mother searched and searched for someone to teach her child. She read a newspaper story written by the famous English author Charles Dickens.

In the story, he wrote about Alexander Graham Bell, the man who invented the telephone and record player.

Charles Dickens told the story of how Alexander Graham Bell was working with The Perkins School. Perkins was a school for the blind. This seemed an answer to her prayer.

Other blind children were learning! She knew her child was trapped. Inside, Helen was a wonderful, bright person.

I think we all have some special talent, a place inside where there is magic. Perhaps we are afraid to show someone who we are. It can seem that no one understands us. We seem to have a secret life, a self we keep hidden away.

Like Helen, parts of me were locked inside. I kept waiting, hoping for someone to find the good parts of me.

I was afraid they would see the bad parts of me. I had vision problems. I had never been to school. I could not read or write, not even my own name. I felt broken. I was angry. I had a fierce temper. I did not want anyone to know this about me.

Chapter 2

Who was Helen Keller?
Why was she important?
Have a sit and I will tell you.

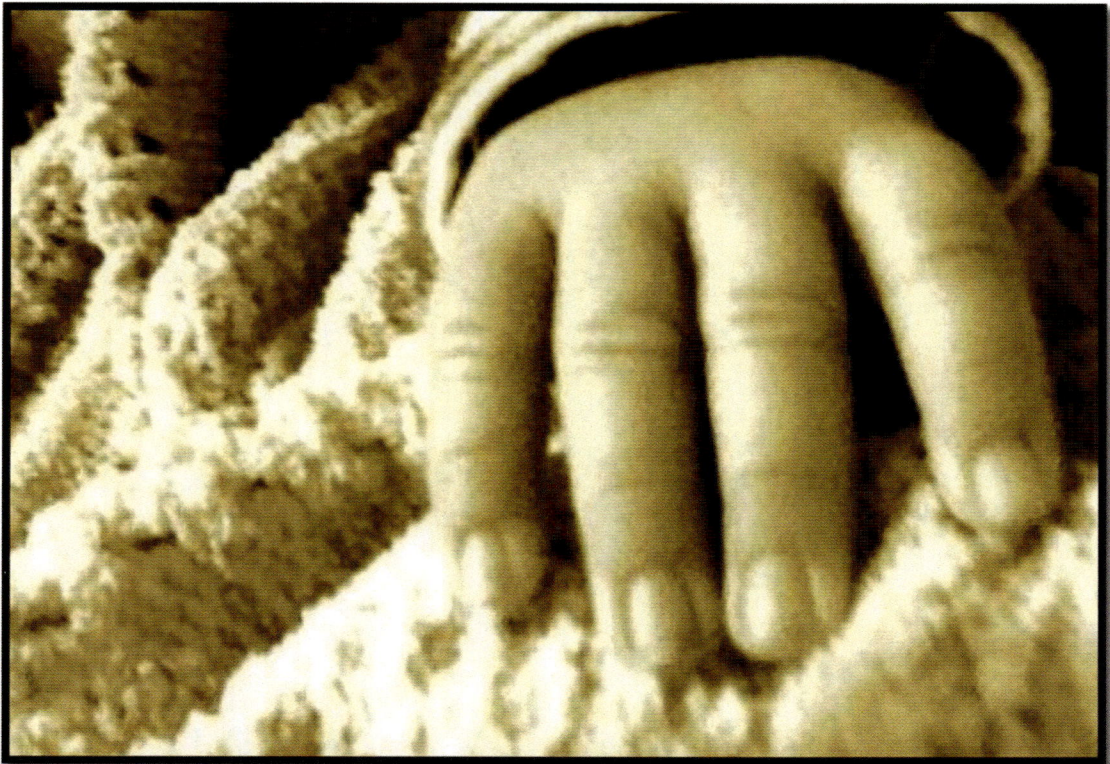

In our nation's capital, Washington, DC, there is a big church. It is our cathedral, The National Cathedral. Many important people are buried there.

This is where Helen and I are buried. Only people who were important in our history are buried there. I was the first woman ever buried at The National Cathedral.

Let me tell you more about my student. Helen was born on June 27, 1880. She was an active, little girl. She was born with hearing and sight.

Her family lived in a white farmhouse, that they called Ivy Green in a small town in Tuscumbia, Alabama. The farmhouse had deep green ivy growing up the side. Ivy Green is now a museum. It is kept to preserve the story of Helen Keller's life.

Helen was a beautiful baby, full of energy. At nineteen months of age she became sick, very, very sick. Everyone thought she would die of the fever. She survived her illness. Her family rejoiced. They rejoiced until they realized the illness had taken away her hearing and vision.

Because of this she could not hear words. She could not see. She was deaf and blind. Frustrated that she could not see or hear, she became a wild child. The only way she could tell people what she needed was through her behaviors.

She would run around the dinner table, feeling with her fingers for the food she wanted. She would grab it off of other people's plates.

Shoving it in her mouth, she would run around grabbing from another plate.

In an effort to tell people what she wanted, she would pull and tug at their clothes! If she did not get what she wanted, she threw a great, fierce temper fit, a tantrum. No one understood her. She could not tell them what she wanted. She could not make anyone listen to her.

Helen said the day we met, March 3, 1887, was her "soul's birthday. "

What do you suppose she meant by that?

We have the day we were born, our birthday. It is celebrated with cake and presents.

There are other days where we make a dream come true or become more of who we are. Those would be our "soul's birthday."

Let me give you an example. Once when I was young, at The Perkins School for the Blind, I was asked to give a speech. (The Perkins School is still there and students are busy studying as you read this!)

Giving that speech felt like my soul's birthday. I stood in front of the other students and the teachers. The teachers were all looking at me, smiling. The students were focused, listening. I felt more myself than ever before.

It was the day where I knew that I loved to speak, to teach. I do believe it may have been my soul's birthday.

That was the day my life changed. It was the day I became who I was on the inside.

I hope you have someone in your life that helps you to be and do your best, which helps you to bring out your magic.

I am famous for being a teacher. Do you think I was all sweet and nice?

Ha.

Helen wrote a book about me. It is titled *Teacher*. Now I would like to tell you my story as her teacher. This will help you to understand how to make a dream come true and your own magic.

Chapter 3

What is your talent?

I know you have magic.

There is something special about everyone. Some of us draw cartoons. Some of us make up stories in our minds, in our imaginations just before we go to sleep at night. Sometimes we have a talent that we keep hidden away.

We may be afraid. Fearing that we will be teased, we tell no one about it. It's locked away. We know it is our special something.

We may need help to find the key. With the right key, we can unlock it. Then the talent, the dream can grow into the something special that we know it can be.

Though deaf and blind, she just needed the right key. As her teacher, I needed to help her find that key.

If she did not have a way to talk, communicate; she would have been trapped inside forever. Finding that key was the magic.

Helen showed me the way. The key for Helen was sign language, communication. From my first day at Ivy Green, I would finger spell, signing to Helen. She always seemed to think this was a game of imitation. She did not connect that the finger movements meant letters, words, and things.

We worked, and worked and tried and tried. Then one day after great effort, it clicked, clicking like a key in a lock.

It was a very hot day. Helen and I were outside exploring. She scampered about the farm enjoying nature. As always, I kept spelling to her. Into her palm with my fingers I would sign out each letter. F-l-o-w-e-r. T-r-e-e. I just kept spelling to her, spelling everything she touched.

In the heat of that day, she found her way over to the well, to get a drink of water. In those times people got water from an outdoor pump that brought water up from the earth. Thirsty, she wanted a drink. I stopped her. I began to spell to her. W-a-t-e-r! W-a-t-e-r, over and over. Spelling to her palm, just like I had done from my very first day there.

This time it was different.

I could feel the change in her fingers. Something happened. She understood. She spelled w-a-t-e-r back to me. The key turned! The door opened! She made the connection. Excited we scurried all about the yard, spelling, naming everything. F-l-o-w-e-r. D-o-g. G-r-a-s-s.

Once she understood that all those motions I was putting in her fingers were letters and words, her fingers were on fire with learning. First she learned the alphabet, then to spell and speak with her hands.

In order to read books, she learned Braille. Braille is a form of printing or writing, used by the blind. Each letter of the alphabet has a raised row of dots. To read Braille you have to touch the page.

In order to read, she learned letters, the alphabet. She used the letter to make words and used the words to make sentences. Helen's fingers allowed her to communicate. They became her voice. Finally, she could let me know her thoughts and dreams.

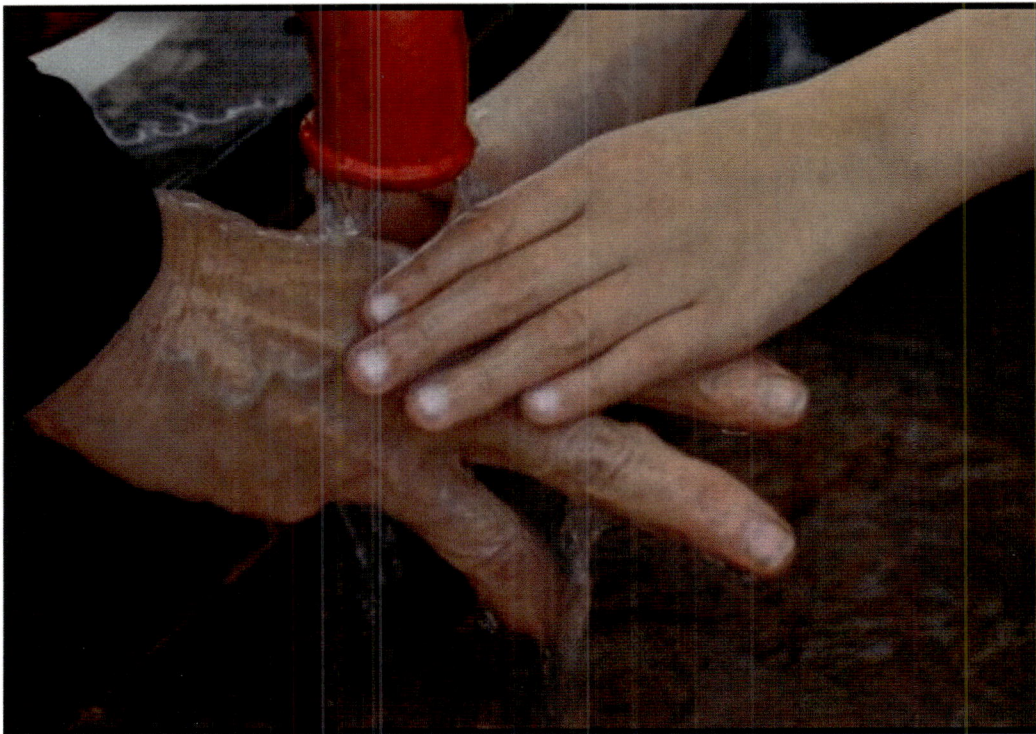

Chapter 4

What person in history would you like to meet?

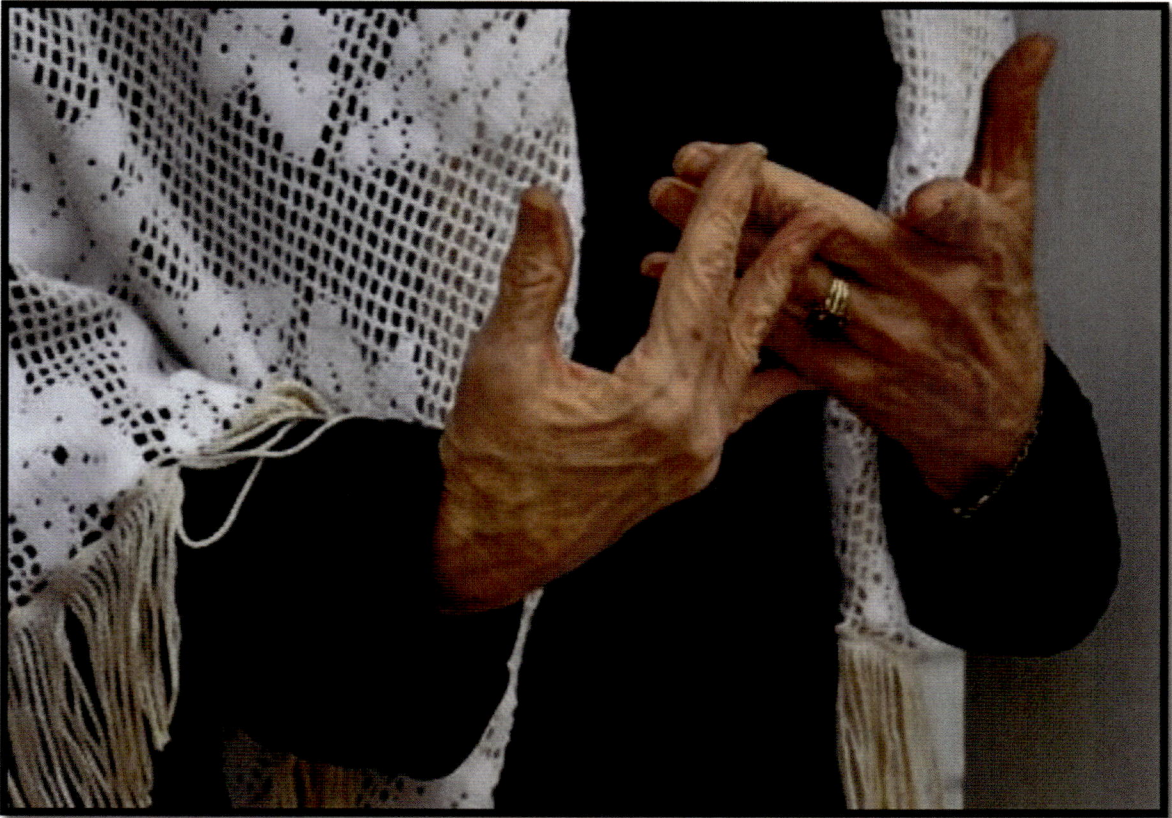

Helen was one of the first persons we know of who had learned to communicate like this. She used this skill to learn and learn.

She traveled everywhere, including, America, England, France and Japan. People the world over wanted to meet Helen. I went with her.

People thought she was a miracle. She had broken out of the prison of deafness and blindness. The key had been found.

Newspapers wrote stories about her. She met many famous people. Mark Twain, Albert Einstein and many presidents were in awe of her.

She went to theaters all over America, sharing her story of hope. People would wait for hours to see her. Helen would stand on stage with the lights beaming down. She would spell into my hand. Talking in that voice that only I could understand. I would speak for her.

She told the story of her life. She wanted the world to know that deaf and blind people could learn. Helen hoped to make the world a better place. And she did.

Helen wrote many books. She wrote the book, *Teacher,* because she wanted everyone to know about me. That is all she ever called me. Teacher! Everyone else called me Annie.

She knew me. But there were many things I did not tell her about myself until she was an adult. I did not tell her the dark, terrible things about my life. I did not tell her the things I wish I could forget. I wanted to protect Helen. I wanted to forget those bad things from my childhood.

Chapter 5

How do you feel when people brag about you?

Teachers love to brag about their students. I bragged about Helen. I was proud of her.

As a teacher I will live forever. Let me explain. By teaching Helen to read and eventually write, a legacy was created. I think all teachers help create a legacy. You are their legacy. When you become all that you can be, all that you dream, a legacy is created.

Remember, in those times children like Helen were just sent away because no one believed they could do anything or have a fulfilling life. Helen changed that.

Helen learned to speak with her hands. She wrote stories. She went to college.

Never before had anyone heard of such a thing as a blind, deaf person learning to speak, read, and write.

It was awe-inspiring. The world began to think differently of deaf, blind people.

Helen continued to amaze. Newspapers featured stories about her. Remember, this was before radios, TV's, or phones.

Helen taught the world that people who could not speak were not dumb. They could learn, once the right key was found. She made us look for her key and for the key of other people. I guess you could say she made us see. She made us see, that all people could learn and achieve with the right key.

Once Helen had a way to express herself, she worked on behalf of others. She worked to help create more tools to assist the deaf and blind. Her accomplishment changed how the world looked at people with disabilities. She worked tirelessly to support the American Federation of the Blind (AFB). This organization began to help injured soldiers returning from World War I. Their goals were to assist in providing education, opportunities, and research for blind people. Still today, 100 years later, AFB helps people with vision issues. The things Helen did made the world better. So, Helen lives forever, and so do I.

What you learn from your teacher you can teach someone else. You will show these things to others. In doing so your teacher will also live forever through you.

Now I would like to tell you a little bit more about me.

My story is about a little girl. One who no one believed in, about a girl who needed to find her magic so she could become the person she was meant to be.

It is true I was easy to irritate. I was easily riled up. Sometimes, I was called Miss Spitfire. Spit! Fire! That makes me seem like a dragon. Spitfire! I always had a spirited nature. I could pop, like a top. I would blow like a kettle's whistle. I had to make noise. That was just my way. Even though I could talk, it seemed nobody listened.

It is a surprise to me that I became a teacher. Teachers are supposed to be patient. Not me! It is not easy to be a child. Grownups seem to forget being small. People forget what it is like to be cooped up in school all day. It can feel like a cage. Children want to run, play, and laugh.

"Teacher." Look it up in the dictionary.

I found twenty meanings for the word teacher! My favorite meaning was "educator." To educate comes from a Latin word that means, "to lead." It means we are to show you the way, give you the path, and help you find the key.

That is what I did with Helen. First, I had to find a way for her to let me lead. With Helen, I discovered the key was signing, speaking with our fingers.

Being her teacher was the most important thing I ever did. "Teacher." Whenever she spoke with me she called me, Teacher. Teacher as if it was my proper name. "Teacher, would you like a walk? Teacher, would you like a tea?"

Most people do not know much about me, and they know very little about their own teachers. What do you know about your teachers?

They know about you. They know how you spell, read, and perhaps how hard multiplication is for you! They seem to know things about your private life, even if you did not tell them. Sometimes you are called to the teacher's desk. In a hushed voice you are asked, "Is everything all right?" How did they know? You wonder if your teacher had peeked into your window before school!

They seem to know that you got hollered at before school, because the dog really did eat your homework. While you were busy hurrying to redo it, your mother was yelling, "Hurry. Hurry." With all the noise, you forgot to eat breakfast.

Then with everything going on, you put on two different socks. Worrying that everyone would notice, you kept leaning over your desk trying to pull your pant legs down to cover your socks. Every thing was going wrong, just like in the book, *Alexander and the Terrible, Horrible, No Good, Very Bad Day.*

You were having a bad day. A very bad day and somehow your teacher just seemed to know. Teachers are supposed to make sure that their students learn all sorts of things. They read you poems. They ask you to write one. They have you practice addition. Those teachers!

Even when you are older, your teacher's voice will stay in your mind.

Even when you are very old you will find yourself remembering the day you felt so proud when your teacher complimented you. Those are the days that make the story of our life better.

Now I will tell you my story. My story does not start with, "Once upon a time." My life was no Fairy Tale. The genre of my early life could probably be called "horror".

Somewhere around 1855, my Ma and Da came to America from Ireland. There had been a great blight that destroyed our crops. There was a famine. There was no food throughout the land. People were dying from hunger. One million Irish people died.

Hoping for a better life, my parents took a ship from Ireland to America. They settled in Massachusetts.

Life however did not get better. Instead, they found a bad dream, a very bad dream, a nightmare.

Ma died of tuberculosis when I was eight. Da liked to drink. He liked his drink and his drinking friends too much to care for us. He could not make any money so we had no food. One day he went missing, on a walk about and never returned. He abandoned us. We were nearly orphans. In the end we were orphans.

We, Jimmie and I, lived with our aunt for a while. This did not last. As you know, I was a mouthy, opinionated child, a spitfire. I had my own ideas. I told everyone what I thought. I had something to say about everything.

Also, I had an eye disease. In part, that is why I was always carrying on. It was very painful. I was mostly blind, seeing only shadows. By the end of my life, I could not see at all.

Jimmie, "me baby brother," as I liked to call him, was very sickly. He had a disease in his bones. His body was all crooked. He looked like a skeleton with skin.

But oh, he had wonderful brown eyes. He had eyes like a golden autumn day.

By the time I was ten I had no Ma. I had no Da. The relatives did not want to care for us. We were too much trouble. These were hard times.

Still there were even harder times to come.

Chapter 6

What has happened in your life that you found hard to talk about?

We were only with our aunt a short time, when a great big black horse-drawn carriage came to her house. The special name of this carriage was the Black Maria. These carriages were used for official police work. Our auntie told us we were taking a trip. She was carrying on, weeping and all.

As we entered the Black Maria, she grabbed hold of us. She held us so tight that I thought I would fall apart. The only other time I saw such sorrow was at Ma's funeral.

That was worst day of my life. Seeing my ma in the casket is like a bad dream I will never forget. Ma was all-stiff, wearing a fancy dress I had never seen before. It seemed as though she was sleeping in the wooden box. I knew she was dead. I knew I would not see her again.

Everyone was wailing and weeping then. Still, I did not cry.

If I did not cry then, I was not going to weep about some carriage ride, even one in a Black Maria. There would be no tears, even if I had no idea where we were going. You would see no tears from me.

Jimmie was seven. I was ten. He was afraid. Maybe he was just fearful of my aunt's wailing. He burrowed into me, tightly clasping my hand.

We were leaving our little town in Massachusetts. I imagined that we were going to the big city of Boston. I imagined we were going to Ireland.

I imagined that we had a lovely granny waiting for us there. The main thing was I was with Jimmie. We were together, my little brother and me. It mattered not where we were going.

We did not go to Boston. Nor did we go to Ireland. We did not find some long lost Granny. We did not find a pretty place. Instead we found a place of terror.

In the middle of the night, the Black Maria crept up a hilly road. We stopped in front of a huge brick building. It was an almshouse called Tewksbury State Home.

Do you know what an almshouse is? An almshouse was a loony bin, an asylum, sort of like a prison.

Back then, almshouses were places where orphans, poor people (paupers we called them), criminals and crazy people were sent to live. Everyone was strewn together. It did not matter if you were a child, a criminal or a mentally ill person. Everyone lived together in the same building.

Now you understand why I did not want Helen to know about that part of my life. Tewksbury was a scary, terrible place.

While we were standing in the great hall, quivering with fear and shaking from the cold, the staff told Jimmie to go to the men's side. They were shooing me off to the women's side.

They were going to separate us. I hollered and carried on. Yes, this was the one time I wept. I carried on, weeping and hollering. I made a scene

They took pity on us. Guess what? They let "me wee brother" stay with me on the women's side. It is not always so terrible to be a Spitfire.

Chapter 7

Where do you put your hard feelings?

Life can get in a jumble. Things can go so wrong. They stick in your throat. They seem to bruise your heart.

Many bad things happened to me when I was a child. Such terrible things, I could not, would not speak of them. Sticking somewhere between my heart and my mouth, I could not get my words out.

All those times when I exploded, when they called me Miss Spitfire because I could blow up so easily, it was because of those bad times. Stuff stayed in me until I blew up! It seemed a boulder had been moved away from the door. Things just came bursting out of me, exploding, spewing all over the place.

Things were held inside until bursting from me, until I made a great fierce noise. Well the story of Jimmie, and what happened to my "wee brother" was the biggest burden of all.

Being at Tewksbury was not easy, but we found our way. I made believe that I was Jimmie's mom, sometimes making sure he got an extra crust of bread. On cold nights, I gave him my blanket, hoping it would warm him and quiet his cough. He was my heart.

There was no privacy at Tewksbury. There was no place to play. Winters were bleak and snowy in the North. Often we went for weeks without going outside. We had no proper clothes.

We found a place to be alone, to play. We found a place where we could be by ourselves. It was the Tewksbury mortuary. The mortuary was the place where they brought the dead bodies when people died there.

In quiet and privacy, Jimmie and I played. Mostly we played school. It really was a game of make believe.

Jimmie and I did not know anything about school. We had never been to school. There was a little school in our town. Because of my vision problems and Jimmie being sickly we were not allowed to go.

The mortuary room became our place. I would pretend that I knew how to read and write. I would be the make believe teacher and Jimmie, my student. I was the teacher, bossing Jimmie, imagining that I knew what I was doing. We made our own little way at Tewksbury.

One morning, I woke to find that Jimmie was not in his place, in the cot next to me.

Where was "me wee brother?" Searching all about the place, I was worried. I ran all over. Maybe he had gotten up in the night to go to the toilet.

A rat! Maybe a rat had bitten him. Maybe he lay on the floor with foam pouring from his mouth, like that dog I had seen back home, in town.

I was frantic, searching, and afraid. I had never let him out of my sight. I went looking everywhere except the one place I was most afraid to find him.

I think I knew all along where he was. Hoping and praying he was not there, it was the last place I looked.

But there he was.

There was Jimmie on the wooden table all-naked in the middle of the mortuary. His little eyes wide open. His beautiful brown eyes with no more sparkle in them. His eyes were just staring, not moving.

Jimmie was dead. He had died in the night.

I never, ever went back to our make believe school in the mortuary. I could not bear to remember to think of Jimmie, "me wee brother," lying all cold and naked there.

Jimmie was my heart. Jimmie was my life. Life without Jimmie was life without a dream.

We have to have dreams. Dreams are what make us what we are.

If you think about it, everything, most everything in life begins with a dream.

Chapter 8

How does someone keep a dream alive?

It is hard to keep dreaming. It is hard to keep believing.

Things happen to keep us from dreaming. We get tempted to shut down our hearts. When we do this, our hearts can get so heavy it seems we cannot move. After Jimmie died, that is what happened to me.

Once Jimmie died, I lost hope.

I needed a new dream. It was more than a dream or a wish.

It was an, "I gotta." You understand this. I gotta! I must!

All else is built on making this one thing happen. I had to get out of Tewksbury! I was starting to die there. Not like Jimmie did in his body, I was starting to die in my dreams. I was starting to die in my heart.

It is important to be exact about our dreams.

My dream was to go to school.

I needed to get out of Tewksbury. To make a dream come true, you have to want it more than anything. You must be willing to do almost anything to make it come true. Well, I did something about my dream.

I, Miss Spitfire, took my future into my own hands. I really surprised myself.

I wanted to go to school in a fierce sort of way. It seems such an ordinary dream. But as I told you, back when I was a child I was not permitted to go to school.

When Ma was sick, I had promised her two things. As she lay there dying, between her cries and prayers, she called me to her bedside. In a voice like a prayer, she whispered, "Annie, please take care of Jimmie."

Then, as a tear fell down her cheek, squeezing my hand, she murmured, as if it were coming from her last breath, "Annie, my love, you must find a way to go to school." Nodding, I squeezed back.

She stared once again to the ceiling, looking, somehow more peaceful.

On her deathbed, I made promises to my mother.

I could no longer take care of "my wee brother." I had failed in that.

But perhaps, it was not too late to keep the other promise. I had to go to school. I had to go for Ma. I had to go for me.

One day some important officials came to Tewksbury. These men in their suits were sent by the governor to check on the conditions there. Stories of the rats and lack of food had riled folks up. The men had been sent to look about the place.

I had heard that one of the men was connected to the Perkins School for the Blind. As you remember, it was the first school in the United States to assist blind children. When I first heard about this school a glimmer of hope was birthed in me. There was a school for people just like me! Who had ever heard of such a thing?

When they arrived at Tewksbury, I crept along the hallway behind the men. Following them as they toured the building, I waited for my chance. This was my one and only chance of a lifetime to get out.

At just the right moment, as I could hardly see, I sort of threw myself into their midst. Flailing about, I cried, "Help me, I am blind. I cannot see. I want to go to school."

I had other wishes, wishing for a dappled pony or some candy. But, my dream of school was different. Some dreams burn deep.

These dreams are the ones that you know will bring more than happiness. These are the key to future dreams. If you can make these dreams come true, life gets better. Certain dreams give birth to more dreams.

Such dreams as these are the magic of us. They seem like a magic seed in the core, heart of our being. These dreams, or hopes are the secret ingredients to the recipe of life. If we can make them happen, everything gets better!

After my fit, begging the men to send me to school, those men took pity on me. Plans were made for me to leave Tewksbury and go to the Perkins School for the Blind. That was the key to all the other hopes that I kept hidden in my heart.

Though not as horrible as Tewksbury, life at Perkins was not easy.

Perkins was a boarding school. Students both lived and went to school there. I had many adjustments to make. The other students mocked me.

Having grown up without a mother, having lived in an asylum and not knowing how to read, write or even sign my own name, they bullied me.

But I had a dream! School and learning were my dream.

Though not always easy, there were some wonderful things about Perkins. The beds were cozy and warm. We had food, lots of tasty food. We even had butter for our bread. During the day, light from the sun shone through the windows, warming me from the inside out.

You remember school was my dream. Without school, without Perkins I would have had to live somewhere like Tewksbury all my livelong days.

School was tough. There were many rules. I had to sit still at all times. The hardest part though was how I was treated.

Even though the students were blind like me, in every other way, we were nothing at all alike. The other students were children of very rich families. They had fine clothes and proper manners. I did not fit in. The other students made sure to let me know this.

I did not have any idea how to act properly. My clothes were raggedy. They mocked and teased me. When they found out I could not read or even write my name, they turned their noses up at me.

Chapter 9

All teachers are patient. True or false?
Tell me what you think?
Who has helped you want to be your best?
Who has helped to make your dream come true?
You know the truth of this.

Maybe some teachers are patient, but not I. I, Annie Sullivan, was not born patient.

I was born straight up stubborn. I stayed that way most of my life. It now seems in ways that it was good that I was stubborn.

Sometimes a thing that seems bad about someone can have a way of turning out to be a good thing.

For example, if had I not been so stubborn with Helen, I think her life would have taken a different turn. Please try to understand those teachers who push and push. They know what you need to succeed when you are a grown up. Teachers know what you need as a foundation to build your dreams.

My being stubborn did help me learn to read. No matter what, I had it in my mind I was going to read. I was going to learn to write. I was not going to let those snobby, rich kids get in my way. Sometimes I would stare at a letter, just look and look, willing it into my head.

I had to get my fear out of the way to help my dream come true.

Maybe that is the other lesson about dreams. We cannot let things, ourselves or other people's taunts or views, get in the way.

The teachers at Perkins helped me. I had so much catching up to do. At the age of fourteen, I had to start like I was a first grader! I had to learn the alphabet, A, B, C, D... and my printing was big, ugly, baby letters.

I was not an easy student. It was not easy for me to be a student. I yearned to be one of those students for whom learning and behaving well came easily.

But alas, I was Miss Spitfire that is what they called me. And Miss Spitfire was who I was.

They stayed on me. The teachers did not give up on me. I did not give up. I did have temper fits now and again.

The teachers did not quit on me. I did not quit on me either. I did learn to read and write. I also learned to finger spell using the American Sign Language system.

There was a famous blind woman at the Perkins School named Laura Bridgeman. She had learned to talk with her fingers and read Braille. She was the first person ever in this country to learn these things. Though she was quite old, I liked talking with her. I was so lonely, her fingers warmed up my lonely heart.

Other good things happened at Perkins. They arranged for me to have surgeries on my eyes. Some of my vision was restored. My eyes pained me less. I could see a bit more.

At Perkins, we had house parents. Mrs. Sophia Hopkins was my wonderful housemother. She taught me how to act like a lady.

"Sit up, dear. Use your napkin. Cover your mouth when you cough."

She said the things that kids with mothers have heard all the time.

Now I had someone to show me the way. Mrs. Hopkins took me to her summer home by the sea. Her cottage was just up the path from the Atlantic Ocean.

The ocean was a delight, entrancing. Ocean air tastes of salt.

The waves crashing on the shore, made me feel like there was music inside of me. I wanted to fly. The sea breezes made me feel like I was dancing without moving. It is so grand!

And knowing that across the Atlantic Ocean was Ireland, made me feel close to my Ma and Da. Ireland was where they were before crossing the sea to come to America.

Looking east, out to sea, I felt both big and small. Through the years, when I missed my Jimmie, I imagined he was at the sea. His body was not at all sick. He was not bent over. All straight and tall, I could just imagine him running, running after a sea gull. Envisioning him, spreading those speckled, freckled arms of his.

Running to the water, laughing, it seemed as if a wave would seize him. I worried he would drown. Then suddenly, he would soar skyward, like a gull, flying. As I looked to the blue, the yonder, trying to follow him, he would disappear.

Maybe, he flew back, back to Ireland. Or perhaps, he became a seagull or an angel, ascending to a cloud, up to the heavens.

When I was little, with Da drinking and Ma ailing, I could not wait to be a grownup. When I grew up I would fix everything.

I would get Ma a warm shawl to take the chill off her. I would make sure she had milk and a little sugar for her tea. I would get a doctor for Jimmie to make him well.

I would find Da a job. I would make lots of money and buy him a fiddle. Then he could play Irish songs and he would not be so sad all the time.

When I was at Tewksbury, I made believe I was a grown-up. Tewksbury was scary. Being a kid was scary. I did not want Jimmie to be any more scared than he already was. I made believe I was brave. Pretending to be a grownup, I would hold Jimmie's hand, sing to him and soothe him. When he cried or was upset I took care of "me little brother." I was his "Little Ma."

While at Perkins, I became a real grown-up. I grew to an age that was considered, "all grown." At twenty, it became time for me to leave Perkins. had graduated, with honors!

It was time for me to make my way in the world. It did not feel like the right time to me. I felt like a baby bird that did not want to leave the nest.

But, I could not stay at Perkins forever. I had to make my way in the world. Now that I was grown, the world still seemed scary to me.

I had no home. I had no family. Leaving Perkins, leaving Sophia Hopkins, my housemother, was a big step. I was not ready to leave the protection of Perkins.

I wondered what I could do? What skills did I have? In those days, there were not many opportunities for women.

I tried to find work. I got a job as a maid. As a maid who was spitfire and partly blind, once again, I did not fit in.

I burned a couple of shirt collars with the iron. The big fine house made me nervous. I was terrible at being a maid. I did not last in that job. I failed at other jobs, too.

Failing is a tough thing. When you fail too often, you can start to believe you are a failure.

Whatever was I supposed to do? Seeming to fit nowhere, I worried what would become of me?

Chapter 10

Think about a magical day in your life. What happened?

Sometimes there are days when life changes almost magically. This is how it happened for me. I told you how Helen's mother searched for a teacher.

That teacher was I. My life changed the day I met Helen.

This was just after the Civil War, the war to free the slaves. The Civil War is sometimes called The War Between the States.

The Northern and Southern parts of our country fought each other. As a person who was from the North, the South seemed a scary place.

Going South was scary. To be a teacher was scary, as scary as when I went to Tewksbury. It is so hard to face the unknown. Leaving Perkins and Mrs. Hopkins, my heart was almost as heavy as when I had lost Jimmie.

I was only ten years older than Helen. In some ways I was still a girl myself. Now, I had to be the responsible one.

It was almost too much. This new life was going to take some serious pretending. I was afraid! Once again, I made believe until I believed in myself.

I took the train and traveled 1,900 miles all by myself. I like to think of it as "the train to destiny."

Upon my arrival, there she was, that wild child, Helen.

I near bolted when I first met Helen. I wanted to run back to the train station and head North. If I was Miss Spitfire, Helen was Miss Volcano. She would explode, all fiery.

As I told you, Helen's thoughts, feelings, ideas and words were trapped inside. Without vision and hearing, Helen was stuck in own sort of jail, her own sort of Tewksbury.

I understood this, as I also had lived in sort of a jail. Going to Perkins School for the Blind was the door that opened to free me from my jail.

The key, the magic to keeping that door open was learning to read and write.

The only way to free Helen was to teach her the same things. When and if I could make her understand that the finger movements were letters, which could come together to make words, she could be free.

Reading and finger spellings were like puzzles. Put it all together and you had language.

I must admit, I was not always patient with Helen. Maybe, I was even stubborn. But more than anything, I was afraid!

Afraid, afraid if I did not teach her, if she did not learn, she would be sent away.

Just like me. Just like Jimmie. She would be sent away to a dark and scary place. On that day, when Helen finally understood, comprehended sign language, hope was born!

Dreams began!

Chapter 11

How do we make a dream come true?

Life is like a book. Life has many chapters. Sometimes life seems the same, day after day. Sometimes, it seems as though we are stuck.

Then in a snap, everything changes. Things change and you can never go back to where you were before. That is how it was with Helen.

On that day when Helen finally understood, she changed, I changed, and perhaps the world changed.

First, I was her teacher. All the thoughts of her mind and all her ideas came into my hand when she signed to me. I spoke for her. Then, I became her voice.

Once she had words, a way to communicate, Helen's personality and mind were on fire! Later, she began to write stories that got published in magazines. Newspapers wrote articles about her.

The entire country was excited about the miracle of how a deaf, blind child learned to speak with her fingers, read and write. Famous people came to see her. If this one little blind, deaf child could learn, maybe other children with disabilities could learn as well.

For forty-nine years, I remained with Helen, her teacher, her friend, and her interpreter. When she spoke to audiences, she spoke to me with her hands. Then I would tell people what it was she had signed to me.

We traveled all around the country. We traveled around the world.

As, "Teacher" and student, we had a very wonderful life together.

The story goes on. Life goes on. There is much more I want to tell you.

There are movies, plays and books about Helen. She wrote a book about her life. The book is titled, *The Story of My Life*.

Helen went to Perkin's School, too. She learned many things there including Braille.

Helen went to college. At first they would not let her in, but you remember, she was no quitter. Not only was the first blind, deaf woman to go to college, to Radcliffe, but she also learned five languages. By the time she graduated, she knew French, German, Greek, and Latin as well as English.

There were bad times. There were good times. We had money troubles. Our home burned down. In the fire, we lost everything we owned.

We had great loves. We lost our loves. We did not dwell on our troubles. They were quiet in our hearts, like I was about Jimmie.

Yet, Helen persevered. There is no better word than this. Persevere. It means to try, and try no matter how hard things get.

Helen worked her whole life long. She was accomplished. What really makes Helen a hero is how she always spoke up for others. She used her special voice, her mind, and her fame to speak on behalf of others.

Helen used her voice to make the world a better place.

Chapter 12

What will happen when you reach your goal?
How do you imagine your life as a grownup?

Communication and language were Helen's keys.

Helen never gave up. Her perseverance and determination were also her magic, her key.

We all have barriers or problems.

I was trapped. Trapped in Tewksbury, trapped by illiteracy. Trapped by how people saw me as stupid, slow, and no good. Like Helen though, I persevered. I was an "overcomer." I would not accept defeat. I triumphed over my barriers. We cannot let problems stop us.

We must persevere. Learning and life are sometimes hard. We all have challenges. It's our dreams that carry us through. Our dreams and hopes make us "overcomers," or achievers.

My life did not have an easy start. If I had given up, I would have never gotten out of Tewksbury. I would have become like the many people who festered and died there.

But, I kept believing, tried and believed some more until I got out of Tewksbury.

As Helen's teacher, I did the same, trying and trying with her until she understood, succeeded. We cannot succeed by quitting.

Have you noticed how teachers often seem to want to have the last word? I know what that's like! I was a student before I was a teacher.

Please let me have a last word with you, to leave you with a big idea to carry with you through life.

Never give up even if it seems everyone else has given up on you. Do not give up, ever!

Are you ready for the magic to begin?

Magic is inside each and every one of us. The magic of try, try again and never give up!

Persevere!

Tell the world what you are thinking by using your imagination

Your magic may be in your writing, drawing, singing, dancing, building or, something else.

You know...your magic.

Share your ideas.

Create your world.

You, make your own magic.

Listen to your dreams.

They are your personal guides.

Believe and persevere!

We all have dreams.

Helen made a believer of me.

I believe in you.

Chapter 13

The Key to Annie's Magic

Now I must tell you about the secret ingredient!

Both Helen and I always wrote journals. Every day we wrote about our lives. Try our way of making this bit of magic, for yourself.

Ponder upon these questions. Write your own story.

Write your own ending! Make it a happy one

The Questions

Remember...

Dream big!

Write your own ending...**now**!

Photography citations:

Pages: cover, 1,9,10,12,17,20,23,33,36,39,42,44 by Cindy Frabutt taken at The Henry Ford/Greenfield Village for the express purpose of this book.

Pages: 4, 8, 28 are from the author's personal photos

Made in the USA
Columbia, SC
17 May 2021

37717546R00031